CHOOSE
JOY

CHOOSE JOY

How To Find Inner Peace Amidst Chaos & Uncertainty

LINDSEY NICOLE

Copyright © 2019 Lindsey Nicole Johnson.

All rights reserved. No part of this document may be reproduced, stored in a retrieval system, or transmitted in any form or by any means, electronic, mechanical, photocopying, recording, or other - except for brief quotations in critical reviews or articles, without prior written permission of the publisher.

ISBN: 978-1-7333148-1-7 (Paperback)

Library of Congress Control Number: 2019911825

Book design by Lindsey Nicole.
Edited by Ellen Johnson.
Page 44, 52 and 56 images by Ellen Johnson printed with permission.
Page 48 image by Liz Warren printed with permission.
Page 102, 106 and 118 images by Alicia Chandler printed with permission.
Author photo by Shannon Edgar.

Printed by 18 Source, in the United States of America.

First printing edition 2019.

18 Source
P.O. Box #1833
Folsom, CA 95763

www.18Source.com

With gratitude to the Infinite Source.

This book is for the rebels, the optimists,
the brave souls who follow their heart,
who relentlessly pursue joy,
who believe in the power of love.

Introduction

"I KNOW HOW TO CHANGE THE WORLD.
STOP TRYING TO CHANGE THE WORLD.
START CHANGING YOURSELF,
AND THE WORLD WILL CHANGE."

- LINDSEY NICOLE -

    We are all more powerful than we know, more spectacular, creative and capable than we can fathom. We are all magnificent creators gifted with life.

    I want you to know that you have the power to change your life. You have the power to change our world. You have the power to choose joy.

    It takes courage and fierce determination

to change oneself. It can feel like the greatest challenge you have ever encountered to change your belief, but honestly it is easier than you might think. It's all about perception. Believe its challenging and it will be. Allow it to be easier and it will be.

The reward for your effort is inner peace. It is a steady peace that you can access during life's challenges. You can be calm and centered amidst chaos, even during times of confusion or destruction.

It is incredible to live this way. Nothing can shake you like it did before. You become powerful beyond measure. When you do not require life to give you what you desire, you are able to live with fulfillment.

Right now, you have everything you need to make the changes that will shift your life. You are not bound by your circumstances. You are only bound by your beliefs.

You can choose to live the life you want. I hope you use the wisdom and insights in this book to support your personal and spiritual growth. I hope these words help you access your own power.

I hope this book reminds you to embrace the uncertainty that accompanies change. I know that when you trust yourself, you will find your own answers.

May you shine brightly and live a life you truly love.

With a great full heart,

Lindsey Nicole

Affirmations

Inner Peace Is My Success.

Dignity Is My Innate State Of Being Worthy.

I Choose Inner Peace Right Now.

I Am Loved Just As I Am.

I Am Gentle With Myself.

I Can Make A New Choice Any Time.

Today, I Choose Joy.

Breathe.

LOVE IS THE ROOT FROM WHICH ALL I DO GROWS

Root of Love

Love is
The foundation of life

Love is the root
From which all I do grows
Infinite in its depths
Unseen by the casual glance

Love allows everything
To expand and thrive

Deep roots of love
Grow strong trees with tall branches
From which new seeds emerge
That grow more
Love

Breathe

Breathe
Now, do it again
Breathe deeply
Fill your chest

Release
Let your breath fall
Along with any tension
You hold in your body

Inhale
Exhale
Feel your chest expand and contract

You can always calm yourself
When you breathe with intention

Embrace Uncertainty

The ocean of uncertainty
Can frighten us when we find ourselves
In over our head
Violently tossed by the waves

You can spend energy fighting the waves
Forgetting the water will hold you

Keep your head to the sky
Lean back with arms open wide
Allow faith to carry you
Even though it feels vulnerable

In the midst of uncertainty
Safety is found
When you act in faith

Peaceful Soul

I am always at peace
Way down deep in my soul

Although the noise of the world
And the thoughts in my head
Sometimes distract me

I know a calm
Deep peace
Lives within my soul

When I breathe I connect easily
With the peace I have within

I can always access
My inner calm

DEEP REST

Deep Rest

Does it seem life is taking a toll
On your precious soul?

What we call depression
Is an invitation to explore
The depth of your inner world

Sometimes we feel depressed
Because what we need is deep rest

Hustle is not the language of the soul

Rest is valuable
Remember that you find
What you are looking for
In the space between

let it be **EASY**

Let It Be Easy

Ease is the ability to move freely
Without restriction
Without limitation

Allow space for grace
For movement
For your own expansion

Go easy on yourself
Allow yourself to have room
From your judgments
And expectations

It can be easy
If you
Let it be easy

Faith Is Demanding

Faith is not easy
Faith is demanding

Faith requires you to drop
Every belief
That does not align
With your highest good

Faith asks you to
Step beyond your desire for certainty
And trust the unseen forces
Of the Universe

Faith is meant to grow
And take root
In every area of your life

EVERYTHING TURNS INTO A BLESSING

Lindsey Nicole

Seek The Blessing

There is a force in our heart
That is greater than any pain

There is a thread that connects every person
Every being, ever fiber of the Universe

From this perspective
Everything is always in perfect order
No one is ever lost
And there is a purpose for every moment

There is always a blessing

Keep searching and you will find
Blessings are revealed
To those who seek

AWAKEN

YOUR

JOY

Awaken Joy

You can always connect with joy
Joy is found deep within

Some of us have pushed our joy aside
Afraid it won't last

It is safe to open your heart to joy
Know that joy
Will never let you down

Joy is always available
And patiently awaits
The invitation of your open heart

Now is the time to
Awaken the joy within

Love Is Everwhere

Love is everywhere
Love is right here
Right now

Have you ever noticed
A little heart on your path?
A love note from the Universe

Stop and notice
You will begin to find reminders
That the Universe loves you
In the most amazing ways

Sometimes the smallest things
Are miracles of love

FIERCE.
BRAVE.
LOVE.

Love Is Fierce

Love is a force
Love is benevolent
Love is always accessible

Love is fierce, yet gentle like water
It can smooth the most jagged rocks

Love is demanding
It asks you to break down every belief
That is not of love
Until you stand completely
In your truth

In a world that idolizes an "illusion of love"
That is both cheap and easy
To be truly aligned in love is brave

ALWAYS ALL GOOD

All Good

Life is all good
There is only one source
From which everything emerges

We learn about opposites as children
Yet in the spiritual world there is no resistance
No opposites
No opposing forces

There is only love

Love is: All Good
Always
In
All Ways

YOU
CHOOSE

You Choose

If you want to feel more in control
Be more intentional with
The power of your attention

Take responsibility for everything
You give your attention to

What you feed grows
Feed your fears... Your fears grow
Feed your limits... Your limitations grow

Feed your gratefulness...
Your life will be full of greatness

It's up to you
You Choose

TRUST YOUR BRAVE HEART

Trust Your Heart

Trust is defined as
A belief in the ability, reliability
Strength or truth
Of someone or something

To be brave
Is to act with courage
The root of the word courage means heart
To be brave
Is to act with heart

Quiet your mind
Access your bravery
Trust your heart
It knows the answers
You seek

FOLLOW YOUR JOY
-LINDSEY NICOLE

Follow Your Joy

What brings you joy?
Do more of whatever comes to mind

Give yourself permission to play
Aim yourself in the direction you want to go

On your quest you might find challenges
Unlike anything you've faced before
That send you into pain, discomfort, or disarray

Know that even in the midst
Of apparent chaos
You can still choose joy

Be relentless in pursuit
Of the joy you want to know

LIVING FROM YOUR HEART IS SIMPLE

It Is Simple

Your heart speaks the language of spirit
Infinite Source knows "how" the miracle
Of your manifested desire will occur

Quiet your mind
Listen to your heart
Release your resistance

Pain will be your guide
It will show you where to look
So you can uncover any thought or belief
That keeps you from your desire

When you truly believe
You can receive
The process is simple

Beyond Comfort

Growth happens outside
Of your comfort zone

The Universe is always expanding
In all directions
Opportunity exists in this moment
That did not exist a moment ago

Growth is a natural process of expansion
Step into the flow of life
Step out of your comfort zone

Grow in all directions
Take your place amongst
The ever expanding
Good of all

Say Yes

Say "Yes"
To the hell yeahs

Say "Yes"
To your dreams

Say "Yes" to all the things
That increase your joy

Say "Yes" to this moment
Even if this is not
The moment you hoped for
It is the only moment you have

Say "Yes"
To Yourself

Your Heart Knows

Trust your heart
It knows all the answers

Your heart is connected
To the Infinite Source of
All intelligence and creation

Listen to the unique
Language of your heart

It speaks in feelings
It speaks in whispers
It speaks in knowing

Listen to your heart
It knows

YOU

You Are The Way

You are the way to love

You are the way to life

You are the way to freedom

You are the way to joy

You are the way to creativity

You are the way to peace

You are the way

The Universe expresses itself

You are the way

Sol-Mate

Sol = Sun

The fire of the sun
Is a steady reflection
The love of Source energy

Unceasing
Unstoppable

Mate = Friend

Become a mate of the sun
Befriend the steady love that is
Always available for you

Be your own sol-mate

Jump In

Don't hold back
On your joy

Dare to jump in
When you are moved
Even if it doesn't make sense
To anyone else

Stop trying to be practical
Stop trying to fit in

Dare to feel fully
And enjoy life

Go ahead
Jump in

Source Of Love

S - Source
O - Of
L - Love

Even in the darkest night
The steady sun shines for you
Right where you are

Rise like the sun
Shine brightly

Let the world see the light
That eminates from within you

You are one with
The Source of Love

SACRED

Sacred

Religions teach only they
Know what is sacred
As if sacredness is limited
By doctrine and dogma

We fear we might be condemned
If we find sacredness
Beyond religion

Everything is sacred
Nature is sacred
Love is sacred
Attention is sacred
Words are sacred

You are sacred

LOOK UP

— Lindsey Nicole —

Look Up

Sometimes we fall
Sometimes we stumble
Sometimes we hit the ground

Sometimes we become aware
Of important things
When we are down

But it is not where
We are meant to stay

Raise your head
Raise your attitude
Raise your awareness

And look up once more

SHAME
LESS

Shame Less

You are enough
You are worthy
You are loved

There is nothing
You could have done differently
The best you can do is accept
That things happen in life
Like it or not

Move forward knowing
"When you know better, you do better"
Shame is a weight you carry
Lighten your load

Feel shame less

WONDER FULL

Wonder Full

Have you ever stared at the stars in wonder?
Looked at the ocean in awe?

Wonder is curiosity
Get more curious
Seek experiences of wonder
Stop calling mediocrity awesome
It is not

If you need help finding wonder
Listen to a young child
They speak the language of wonder

Life can be full of wonder
When you think
In curiosity

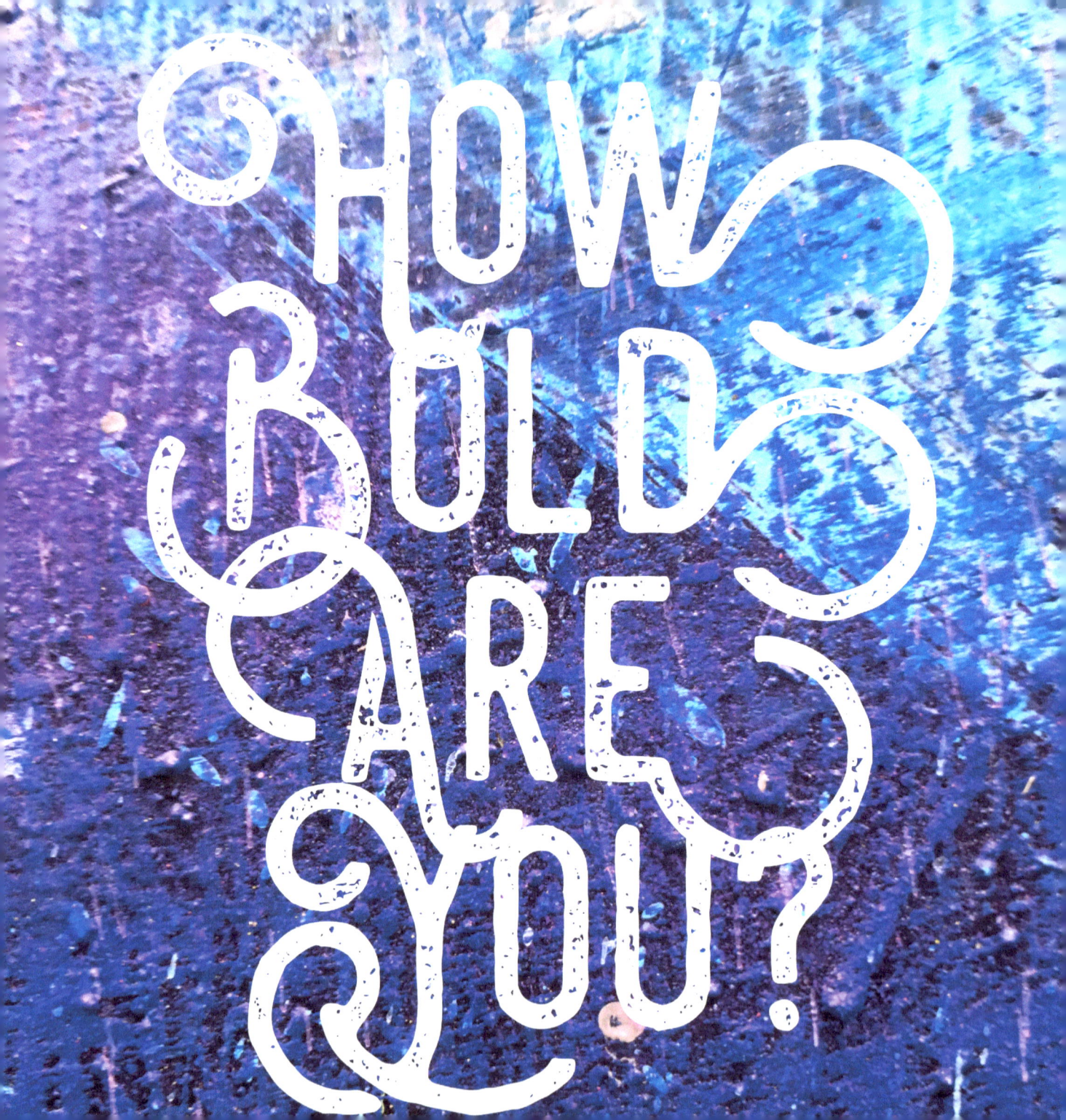

Be Bold

You are meant for greatness
Everyone is meant for greatness

Stop holding yourself back
Stop dimming your light
So that others may shine

This world is unlimited
In it's ability to provide for you

Stand in Your Truth
Dare to dream audaciously
Resolve to do everything you can
Persist when it gets hard

Be Bold - Right Now

Joy Rebel

In a world that places
So much value
On pain and suffering
To choose joy when things
Do not go as you want
Is an act of rebellion

Like the eye of a hurricane
Joy knows calm can be found
In the middle of chaos

Joy is relentlessly optimistic
Joy knows the root of its power
Is found in its infinite depths

True Rebels Choose Joy

imagination + action = magic

Predictable Magic

Magic is not limited to
The fantastical worlds of wizards
Fairies and gnomes

There is a process
That allows "magic" to manifest
Imagination is the
Idea of things to come
Action is motion

Action taken in the direction of a dream
Is the process
That allows something new
To be created from nothing

Imagination + Action = Magic

BOUNDARIES
MOVE

Boundaries Move

Have you ever looked
At a map from the past?
Did you notice that the boarders
Of entire countries have moved?

We too must change
As we move through life

Our boundaries are not fixed
Like a line drawn in the sand
We move in relation to each other
We adapt to each moment
To each interaction

You choose how and when
Your boundaries move

LIFE IS A CANVAS

PAINT WHAT YOU WANT

Blank Canvas

With each new day
In every moment
There is a blank canvas
Open to all possibilities

You fill in each day with the colors
Of your thoughts and emotions

In every moment you paint
The canvas of your life
With the words
Feelings and actions
You choose

Be mindful of the life you want
The brush is in your hand

LIMIT LESS

Limit Less

The Universe is infinite
Limitless abounds

In this timeless expanse
Every possibility
Is yours, right now

Decide in this moment
To limit yourself less
Choose to believe the impossible

You are worthy to receive
Everything that will propel you
Into the life you desire

You are limitless

What
Differently
We
Saw
Things

Think Different

What if we saw "different" differently?

What if our differences brought us together?
Increased our understanding

What if different meant beautiful
Valuable and meaningful?

What if different was necessary?

What if different had no context
Of being bad or wrong?

What if you changed the world
By embracing everything
That makes you different?

CHOICES:
YOU CAN ALWAYS MAKE
A NEW CHOICE

A New Choice

You always have the opportunity
To make a new choice
You are never stuck
In your circumstances
With no way out

No matter the challenges
No matter the conditions
No matter what anyone says

You cannot change others
You can only change yourself

You can shift your mindset
You can choose your response
You can make a new choice

RELENTLESS *Optimism* & RESILIENT *Joy*

Relentless + Resilient

There is great power in
Relentless optimism

Practice being relentlessly optimistic
When you face anything
That appears to be evidence
Your fears are true

Your fears are illusions
Like shadows they dissolve
In the presence of sunlight

Joy is resilient
Joy weathers every storm

Be relentless in your pursuit of joy

Love(d)

Love is in you
Even if you don't feel it
No matter your current mood
Love is in you

Emotions change like
The direction of the wind
Invisible to the naked eye
You may not see
The love that is yours

Yet
Love is yours
Every moment of every day
You are love
You are loved

Imperfect

I'mPerfect

Imperfection is perfection

If you look you will find
You are imperfectly perfect
Just as you are

Perfection is the idea
That something or someone is
Flawless and complete

Sometimes we strive for perfection
Thinking it will save us from pain

The Universe is made of energy
Ever expanding and always evolving
Nothing is ever complete

Joy More. Fear Less.

Joy is a choice
Fear is a choice

You feed each with
The power of your attention
Be mindful of what you want
And feed only the thoughts
That align with your desire

Your body will follow
Your mind will follow
Your life will follow

You hold the power
To create your life
Choose Well

Love Over Fear

Love over fear

Love over pain

Love over illness

Love over hate

Love over despair

Love over abuse

Love over conflict

Love over, and over,

And over again

SILENT

LISTEN

Silent Listen

Silent and listen
Have the same letters
And the same energy

Silence is the quiet space in between
Thoughts that cloud our mind

Listening is a space of connection
Shared between two people
Listening can also happen between
Yourself and your higher being

Spend time listening to silence
You will find it is not empty

Silence is full of love

BE**LIE**VE

BELIEVE

What if there is a LIE
In the middle of all of our beliefs?

What if the lie doesn't come
From a place of malice
Rather it is a byproduct
Of our humanity?

We all have a cognitive bias that
Validates our own beliefs
It makes us feel safe in a world
That can change at any moment

Be flexible in your beliefs
You don't have to believe
Everything you think

LOVE
YOURSELF
FIRST

Love Yourself First

What if love was
The language you spoke?

What if you gave yourself
An equal portion
Of the love you give others?

What if you loved deeply
And held strong boundaries?

What if you judged yourself less?

What if you talked to yourself
Like someone you loved?

What if you loved yourself first?

TO BE FEARLESS FEAR LESS

Fear Less

There is an equation
To fearlessness

To Be Fearless
Fear Less

There is no use
In trying to eliminate
All your fears

There is no use
In making decisions
Based in fear

The key is to
Fear Less

YOU
CHOOSE
CHOOSE
YOU

You Choose You

Your uniqueness matters

You matter
Just as you are

You are enough
Just as you are

You are love(d)
Just as you are

No one is above you
No one is beneath you

You always have a choice
Choose you

Enough

Enough.

I am enough

You are enough

We are enough

Love is enough

There is enough

I've had enough

You are enough

I am enough

DIGNITY

Dignity

Dignity is your innate
State of being worthy

Dignity means you are worthy
Just as you are
And for all that you are not

Dignity cannot be achieved
Your worth can never be measured

Realize that dignity is your birthright
Equally given to all people.

Dignity for one is
Dignity for all

Stand In Your Truth

Own your power
Stand in your truth

Know what is yours to do
Act from a place of calm knowing

If you don't know what your truth is
Allow yourself time and space
Free of judgment
Your truth will emerge naturally
From deep within you

When you align yourself
And your highest good
You will then
Stand in your truth

BE

Be here
Right now

Allow allow allow
Yourself to be
Present to this moment
Without judgment
Of the feelings
You have

Be with
Your emotions
As they arise
Love them just
As they are

WHOLE NESS

Wholeness Is Natural

All natural systems
Exist in equilibrium
Wholeness is our
Natural state of being

Whole means complete
Unbroken, undamaged, altogether

Everything in nature
Exists in wholeness

You too exist in wholeness
Even in your perceived imperfection
You are whole
You are part of
The wholeness of nature

STRONG
ROOTS

Strong Roots

Strong Roots

Grow Tall Trees

With Strong Branches

That Bloom With Flowers

Which Bear Fruit

And Drop Seeds

That Become New Trees

With Strong Roots

inner peace is my success

Peace Is My Success

Inner Peace
Is a sense of ease
Deep in your heart

Success is achievement of a goal
What is it you want to succeed in?

Will you choose to succeed at a life
Lived in stress and anxiety?

Will you choose to live with peace
As your benchmark for success?

Inner peace is a calm knowing
You are always where
You are meant to be

Let's Connect

Get Your Bonus Download
"10 Keys To Joy"

www.LindseyNicole.co/joy

Instagram

@LindseyNicole.co

Online

www.LindseyNicole.co

Order Books or Products

www.LindseyNicole.co/buy

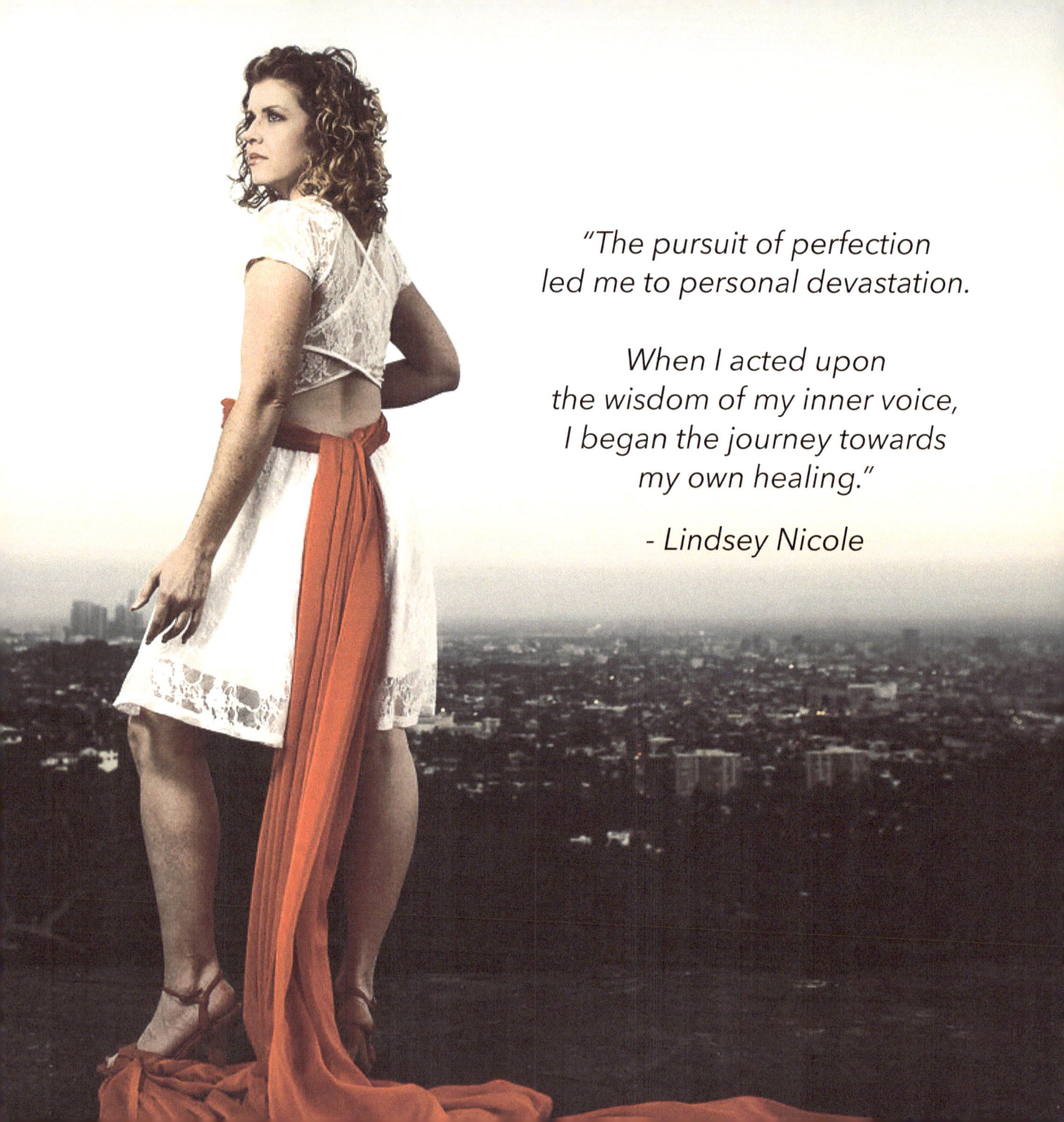

About The Author

Lindsey Nicole is an optimist who believes in dignity for all. She encourages people to redefine success so they can become more passionate, purposeful and fulfilled.

Lindsey knows that light can emerge from very dark times. After enduring a verbally and emotionally abusive relationship for nearly a decade, she found herself feeling broken, hopeless and lost. Eventually, Lindsey decided she wanted to know inner peace.

As she aimed herself toward joy, Lindsey faced the chaos and uncertainty that accompanied divorce, depression, the diagnosis of her son with autism and bankruptcy. These challenges eventually led her to experience deep inner peace.

Lindsey lives in Northern California with her family. She finds joy hosting a radio show with her son and can often be found dancing to a country song.

www.ingramcontent.com/pod-product-compliance
Lightning Source LLC
Chambersburg PA
CBHW041124070526
44584CB00003B/271